More Fruit

Georges André

CHAPTER TWO
Plumstead, London

ISBN 0 947588 24 8

Bible quotations taken from the Authorized Version
(Crown copyright).

Distributors:
Africa: Word of Truth, PO Box 1126, Kaduna, Nigeria.
Australia & New Zealand: Geelong Christian Literature,
11 Barwon Blvd., Highton, Victoria 3216, Australia.
Canada: Believers Bookshelf, 893 Attwood Place, Kingston, Ontario,
Canada K7P 1NP.
The Bible Treasury Book Store Inc. 46 Queen Street, Dartmouth,
Nova Scotia B2Y 1G1.
Christian Messenger, 45 William Street, Ottawa, Ontario.
Eire & Northern Ireland: Words of Truth, PO Box 147, Belfast BT8 47T.
England & Scotland: Chapter Two Bookshop,
199 Plumstead Common Road, London SE18 2UR.
Central Bible Hammond Trust Ltd., 30 South Road, Wooler,
Northumberland NE71 6SP.
India: R. Fernandes, 3 Chuim Khar, Bombay, 400–052.
U.S.A.: Believers Bookshelf Inc., PO Box 261, Sunbury,
Pennsylvania 17801.

Cover design: by courtesy of Beroa-Verlag, Zurich, Switzerland.

Production and printing in England for
CHAPTER TWO
95 Genesta Road, Plumstead, London SE18 3EX by
Nuprint Ltd, Harpenden, Herts AL5 4SE

Contents

Foreword

Do you long to be fruitful in your Christian life? What is the secret of fruit-bearing which truly glorifies God? Fruit bearing is not the exercise of gift, nor service, nor abundant labours for Christ. The Christian is exhorted to 'walk worthily of the Lord unto all well-pleasing, bearing fruit in every good work' (Col 1:10). This clearly shows that good works and bearing fruit are linked but we must distinguish between them. The natural man can do very many good works but in none will there be found any fruit for God.

Fruit must be the expression of Christ in the believer's life. The fruit of the Spirit is love, joy, peace, longsuffering, gentleness, goodness, faithfulness, meekness, temperance (Gal 5:22,23). Don't these nine wonderful flavours give a beautiful description of Christ as He passed through this world in humiliation? If such features are seen in Christians, then the result will be the reproduction of Christ in His people. It is evidently still the Father's intention to have Christ formed in us—in the world where the Lord Jesus was hated and rejected. What a privilege to have the Father graciously intervening to bring about more fruit in our lives.

We pray that the God and Father of our Lord Jesus Christ will be graciously pleased to use this book for His own purposes and glory.

E.N.C., London.

Introduction

Our subject, at first sight, appears stern, and yet how up-to-date it is! Often young people, and those not so young, wonder, 'Why has God allowed such a happening in my life? Why have I failed my exams? Why is my mother so ill? Why this bereavement?'

To such questions two main types of reply are given: Islam's fatalistic one: 'It is written; one must accept it and submit to it; it is inevitable'. Then the quite different Christian answer: 'What dost Thou wish to teach me?' Not a passive answer, but an active acceptance of that which God allows in the life of His own, in order to produce in it fruit that may be for His glory.

Discipline is an element of the work God undertakes in each one of His children, with a purpose of grace that will be for His glory: 'The LORD will perfect that which concerneth me' (Psalm 138:8). 'He is in one mind...he performeth the thing that is appointed for me' (Job 23:13,14). As the Apostle says: 'He which hath begun a good work in you will perform it until the day of Jesus Christ' (Phil 1:6). Hebrews 13:21 confirms: 'Working in you that which is wellpleasing in his sight, through Jesus Christ'.

Romans 8:28 tells us that 'all things', not only the nice ones and the easy ones, 'work together for good to them that love God'.

John 15:1,2 speaks to us of the Father as the husbandman who 'purgeth' the fruit-bearing branch, 'that it may bring forth more fruit'. This is the fruit that Philippians 1:11 speaks of: 'Being filled with the fruits of righteousness, which are by Jesus Christ, unto the glory and praise of God'. We are not concerned with service here, the result of activity for the Lord, but with moral fruit which is produced in us by the life of God, under the action of the Holy Spirit.

Hebrews 12:5–11 in particular, presents the subject which is to occupy us. It is important to read the passage in full.

And ye have forgotten the exhortation which speaketh unto you as unto children, My son, despise not thou the chastening of the Lord, nor faint when thou art rebuked of him: for whom the Lord loveth he chasteneth, and scourgeth every son whom he receiveth.

If ye endure chastening, God dealeth with you as with sons; for what son is he whom the father chasteneth not? But if ye be without chastisement, whereof all are partakers, then are ye bastards, and not sons.

Furthermore we have had fathers of our flesh which corrected us, and we gave them reverence: shall we not much rather be in subjection unto the Father of spirits, and live? For they verily for a few days chastened us after their own pleasure; but he for our profit, that we might be partakers of his holiness. Now no chastening for the present seemeth to be joyous, but grievous: nevertheless afterward it yieldeth the peaceable fruit of righteousness unto them which are exercised thereby.

What is discipline?

The Greek word for 'discipline' comes from the word *paideia*, derived from *pais* (child), which is found in such English words as pedagogue, pediatrician. Three meanings for this word may be discerned in the Scriptures:

To bring up, to educate, to instruct

It is so in Acts 22:3 where the Apostle Paul recalls that he has been 'brought up' at the feet of Gamaliel.

In Titus 2:12, we find the grace that 'teaches' us. Its effect is not an intellectual teaching, but a training that is altogether practical through life: 'denying ungodliness and worldly lusts, we should live soberly, righteously and godly'. What education!

In 2 Timothy 2:25 it is a matter of 'instructing' in meekness those who oppose themselves. Not just a dogmatic teaching, but all that implies an education, a discipline, in order that the one who is opposed to divine thought should be brought back to 'do His will'.

Finally, in 2 Timothy 3:16, we find that Scripture is profitable, among other things, for 'instruction' in righteousness; practical teaching if ever there was!

In Ephesians 6:4 we again find the same word, where parents are exhorted to 'bring up' their children (not to let them grow up!) in the nurture and admonition of the Lord. This is the usual bearing of the word 'discipline', which implies not only education, but also correction.

To correct

The book of Proverbs brings this meaning before us many times (3:11–12; 20:30; 29:15; etc) not merely instruction, rebuke, but also correction, the 'rod'. Such correction implies pain, hardness; Hebrews 12:11 describes it as 'grievous'.

The Father must 'purge' the branch, because there are things that must be taken away. The Father's love, not His anger, is at the root of such discipline. Hebrews

12 emphasizes it: 'Whom the Lord *loveth* He chasteneth'; the Father trains His sons because they are His, not so that they may become such. And let us not forget that this paternal discipline is applied to each one: 'all are partakers' (v.8).

What is its object? Verse 10 tells us, 'for our profit', and 'that we might be partakers of his holiness'. Not a holiness we have to attain, but that of which He has made us partakers, and which He calls on us to reproduce in our lives.

Fathers who discipline their children are 'respected' by them. To let young children please themselves surely does not lead them into a disposition towards their parents which is appropriate. The discipline of the 'Father of spirits' produces 'subjection' (v.9). It leads us to say, as did the Lord Jesus in Matthew 11:26: 'Even so, Father...'. Or, as He will Himself say at the most solemn, most sorrowful hour of His life, 'Thy will be done'. This is the teaching of Romans 12:2, 'that ye may prove what is that good, and acceptable, and perfect will of God'.

When the child of God is under his Father's discipline, two dangers present themselves to him: 'Despise not thou the chastening of the Lord' (v.5). To despise discipline is not to pay attention to it, to think it will soon come to an end; it is also to shield oneself from it: stoicism; or yet to accept it with passive resignation: fatalism.

The other danger is to lose courage, to 'faint' (v.5). Proverbs 24:10 puts it like this: 'If thou faint in the day of adversity, thy strength is small'. One may, as a preacher has said, lose oneself in a forest of 'why?'. One may also, as in Isaiah 40:27, believe that 'my judgment is passed over from my God', and think that the Lord forgets us.

What are we to do? Right at the outset to ask the Lord

to deliver us from discouraging thoughts. Then to search in the Word for the promises He makes us in view of difficult times. Finally, to consider the numerous exhortations of Scripture relating to testing. For example, Daniel 10:19: 'O man greatly beloved, fear not: peace be unto thee, be strong, yea, be strong. And when he had spoken unto me, I was strengthened'. Then again, Isaiah 7:4 'Take heed and be quiet; fear not, neither be fainthearted'. Let us remember the voice of the Lord Jesus to those who were struggling to row in the storm, 'Be of good courage; it is I, be not afraid'. (See article by CHM: Christ in the vessel, misc. writings Vol. 6.) Hebrews 13:5–6 adds, 'He hath said, I will never leave thee, nor forsake thee; so that we may boldly say, The Lord is my helper, and I will not fear what man shall do unto me'. Let us again read Psalm 94:19: 'In the multitude of my thoughts within me, thy comforts delight my soul'. If on the other hand we are unwilling to accept the trial from our Father's hand, bitterness is the result.

Even so, the Word recognises that discipline, for the present, is, or at least seems to be, a matter of sorrow. Later on, it yields the peaceable fruit of righteousness to them that are exercised by it (Heb 12:11). But being 'exercised' does matter, finding out what the Lord wishes to say to us by this trial, and what needs to be taken away from us, given up, judged. With the temptation He will also make a way of escape, 1 Corinthians 10:13 tells us, for He is faithful. But He wants us to take these things seriously, to consider them in His presence and in His light.

How do our hearts answer to the Father's heart, who afflicts us in His desire to see us produce fruit? Do we know how to express to Him our gratitude for the result at which He is aiming? And if the trial remains a mystery, we can abandon ourselves to His grace:

'Underneath are the everlasting arms' (Deut 33:27).

Fruit produced by discipline, peaceable fruit, enables us to help others who are passing through trial: 'Wherefore lift up the hands which hang down, and the feeble knees' (Heb 12:12). After having experienced the Father's faithfulness and love, let us be always ready to come to the aid of those who might lose courage when their turn comes to pass through suffering: 'Comfort the feebleminded, support the weak' (1 Thess 5:14; 2 Cor 1:4).

To chastise

The Greek verb *paideuo*, in certain passages, goes that far. For example in 1 Corinthians 11:32, 'When we are judged, we are *chastened* of the Lord, that we should not be condemned with the world'. In this instance, discipline assumes the character of chastisement, because there has been an evil, more or less serious, that has been left unjudged, and that has been allowed to drag on. This chastisement would have been spared to us if we had recognised our fault and had judged its causes. Again, it is the Lord's love which chastises, so that we should not be 'condemned'.

The thought of self-judgment leads David to say, at the end of Psalm 139, 'Search me, O God, and know my heart;... and see if there be any wicked way in me'. At the beginning of the Psalm it was, 'Thou knowest...' (vv.2,3); the conclusion, 'Search me', so as to accompany the divine scrutiny right to the depths of our heart. Sometimes a distressing experience, of which Job could say, 'Is it good that he should search you out?' (13:9). But will not such an exercise allow us to be led 'in the way everlasting'?

In Revelation 3:19, as the last exhortation to Laodicea, which has drawn so far away from the Lord, He again says, 'As many as *I love* I rebuke and chasten; be zealous therefore and repent'.

Not every trial is a chastisement. The disciplinary ways of God are exercised in training, in correction, but always with a view to producing a good outcome, and to deepening the spiritual life of His children. Other trials are positively 'for the glory of God'. Such was the case of the man born blind in John 9:3 and in that of Lazarus in John 11:4. In other instances, a testimony for the Lord's glory can be rendered by those who experience great suffering.

To do thee good at thy latter end

Chapter 8 of Deuteronomy, notably verses 2–6 and 14—17, illustrates, in Israel's history, the whole scope of discipline. 'These things happened unto them for ensamples', says 1 Corinthians 10:11. It is important therefore to consider them. The LORD says to His people, 'Thou shalt remember all the way which the LORD thy God led thee...in the wilderness'. There are milestones in life: a birthday, the end of the year, a day's solitude, when we are called to consider the way by which we have been led. Two kinds of experience may have marked the road travelled. On the one hand, trials 'to humble thee, and to prove thee, to know what was in thine heart'. On the other hand, all the care of divine providence: 'He fed thee with manna...thy raiment waxed not old upon thee, neither did thy foot swell...who brought thee forth water out of the rock of flint'.

This paternal discipline, as also the benefits of His providence, have a very precise goal:

lest 'thine heart be lifted up' (v.14);
Lest 'thou forget the LORD thy God' (v.14);
lest 'thou say in thine heart, My power and the might

of mine hand hath gotten me this wealth' (v.17).

Another purpose of trial is emphasized in verse 3:
'He suffered thee to hunger...that he might make thee
know that...by every word that proceedeth out of the
mouth of the LORD doth man live'. To be hungry
implies being unsatisfied, in need, discontented,
which God allows in order to make us feel that only
spiritual things can satisfy this 'hunger'. This is the
experience of 2 Corinthians 4:16–18: 'We faint not...
we look not at the things which are seen; for the things
which are seen are temporal, but the things which are
not seen are eternal'.

The conclusion of the whole chapter is that of our
heading, 'To do thee good at thy latter end' (v.16).
Humiliation, trial, hunger, had but one aim, to bring to
fruition the work which God had undertaken in their
heart. The Psalmist could say, 'It is good for me that I
have been afflicted' (Ps 119:71); 'God who fulfils his
purpose for me' (Ps 57:2 RSV). Is not the 'rod' in the
Shepherd's hand (to bring back the straying sheep) an
instrument of comfort?

We shall endeavour to illustrate this discipline by
various biblical examples: Here we shall consider in
particular:

JOB: Discipline in order to know one's own heart

ELIJAH, JONAH, JOHN MARK: Discipline and
    restoration to service

ELI, ELIMELECH and NAOMI, ABRAHAM:
    Discipline in the family

THE RECHABITES (Jer 35): Personal discipline,
    emphasized by 1 Corinthians 9:24–27 and
    11:31–32

PAUL: Preventive discipline, with regard to the
    ministry.

1

JOB

Discipline in order to know one's own heart

One of the objects of the wilderness journey was to bring the people to 'know what was in their heart' (Deut 8:2), this heart that God alone really searches: 'the heart is deceitful above all things, and desperately wicked, who can know it? I the LORD search the heart, I try the reins, even to give every man according to his ways' (Jer 17:9–10). This is why the psalmist prayed to God to search his heart and to know his thoughts, so that the wicked way that could be found in him might give place to the way everlasting.

Such was Hezekiah's experience when, at the peak of is career, 'God left him, to try him, that he might know all that was in his heart' (2 Chron 32:31). Above all, Job's experience. The Word of God consecrates a whole book to teach us that self-satisfaction (Job 33:9) must give way to self-judgment and at the same time surrender to grace (42:6).

Let us begin by stressing that the discipline to which Job was subjected was not a punishment, as his friends erroneously believed. God made use of it to bring into focus His own righteousness which was hidden in His heart, the only means of bringing Job into real blessing. Speaking of Job, James tells us, 'Ye have seen the end of the Lord, that the Lord is very pitiful and of tender mercy'.

Job blessed

The Word says over and over that Job was a perfect and upright man, fearing God and eschewing evil. The LORD Himself calls him 'my servant'. He was blessed in his family: his seven sons and three daughters appear to have had good relations amongst themselves. He was successful in his undertakings. His livestock multiplied, his crops prospered. His moral life was exemplary; he was faithful; he took care of the orphan and of the widow; he was hospitable. He was altogether a man worthy of respect (29:7 *et seq*).

What then was lacking in this patriarch? Even in trouble he attributes to God nothing untoward; he does not sin with his lips; he maintains his own integrity, but...he was only too much aware of it: 'My righteousness I hold fast, and will not let it go; my heart shall not reproach me so long as I live' (27:6)! And again, 'I am clean without transgression, I am innocent; neither is there iniquity in me' (33:9).

Of his children Job said, 'It may be that my sons have sinned, and cursed God in their hearts' (1:5). It would not have entered his thoughts that he himself could have spoken against God.

How then will the LORD operate in order to lead Job to know the depth of his heart? This is the theme of the whole book, thirty-nine chapters, much more than He takes to bring before us the life of Abraham or of Joseph!

Job tested (1:13–22)

Trials are about to overtake Job. He will be stripped of his possessions. He is going to be deeply touched in his affections by the death of his children. But his attitude remains quite remarkable: 'The LORD gave, and the LORD hath taken away; blessed be the name of the LORD'. He is then touched in his body; sickness overwhelms him, 'sore boils from the sole of his foot unto his crown'. The enemy employs his wife to prompt him to curse God. But Job stands firm and does not sin with his lips.

There is no question here of a series of tragic accidents, or an accumulation of misfortunes. No, the Word shows us that God is directing it all. While events behind the scenes are unveiled a little to our eyes, it is He who directs Satan's attention to Job, at the same time imposing limits on the enemy's power (1 Cor 10:13). Is Job, despite all that is to be revealed of his inner self, going to glorify God so far as Satan is concerned? In 1 Corinthians 4:9, the apostles are made a spectacle even for the angels, witness to their faith to the glory of God, just as were the three young Hebrews in the fiery furnace.

Satan is 'the accuser of the brethren' (Rev 12:10). He is our 'adversary' (1 Peter 5:8). He provokes God against Job (1:9–11; 2:4–5). He 'provokes' David to number Israel (1 Chron 21:1). He 'resists' Joshua the High Priest (Zech 3:1). He 'desires to sift' Simon Peter (Luke 22:31). Notwithstanding, he is only an agent in the hands of the Lord; at the end of the trial he disappears, leaving the saint before God: Job in chapter 42, David at Ornan's threshing floor, Joshua clothed with a change of raiment, Peter fully restored.

But when he has established himself in the heart, the Adversary does not let go of his prey, as in the case of Judas (John 13:27) and Ananias (Acts 5:3). God gave Paul a 'messenger of Satan to buffet him'; despite this, and by the action of divine grace, his communion with God was maintained all his life (2 Cor 12:7).

Job's reaction to trial is remarkable; but his story could not end there. God wanted to give him a double blessing, to reveal Himself to him, to manifest His grace and to give true rest to this troubled soul (3:25–26). Job was a picked man, an isolated individual, with whom God was occupied in grace, outside of His chosen people, to mould him and to bring him nearer to Himself.

The three friends

Job's wife urges him to curse God. His friends meet together 'to mourn with him and to comfort him'. In spite of all their good intentions, they are going to push him to the limit. They do not enter at all into God's plan, and, set in their point of view, are ever more entangled in their erroneous statements.

What an appropriate example to make us prudent when we visit friends in trouble! One is easily inclined to judge instead of being reserved in one's appreciation of the motives behind the discipline that God allows to our brother. How necessary it is to be led by the Spirit of God, step by step, word upon word; first to listen patiently; then, looking to the Lord, to open His Word.

The friends come to 'mourn' with Job, to keep him occupied with himself. This is a snare. If someone is experiencing trial, it is not a matter for pity, or perhaps to echo his cries of 'why?' But much rather 'to comfort him' as Job's brothers and sisters will do afterwards (42:11), and above all, like Elihu, to direct his thoughts and his heart towards God. For seven days and seven nights, confronted with this calamity, the friends remain dumb, after a profusion of weeping, having rent their garments and thrown dust on their heads. 'They saw that his grief was very great'.

Before this silence, charged with rebuke, Job cannot

contain himself. He explodes (3 *et seq*). Why? Why? Why? He does not kick against the circumstances, he accepts them from the hand of God, but against the motives for this trial, which he cannot discern, and which he finds unjust. Hence arise his torment and his cries of 'Why?'

Twenty-nine chapters bring before us the patriarch and his friends discussing, arguing, striving. The three say and keep saying, 'God is punishing you because you have sinned'. Job replies: 'I am pure; I have not committed any iniquity.' Pushed to the limit, he accuses God: 'He is unfair; He adds to my iniquity' (14:17).

The tone of the debate grows stronger, sharper, bringing to light that self-righteousness, that self-satisfaction, that spiritual pride which were in the depth of Job's heart. He is going to recall all his good actions (29), all the evil he has been able to avoid; esteeming that God is punishing him wrongly, he asks to be able to speak to Him: 'I would declare unto him the number of my steps; as a prince would I go near unto him' (31:37).

After this long and apparently useless argument, one single solution is arrived at: 'The words of Job are ended' (31:40). That is the first step towards restoration: to hold one's peace.

Elihu

During the long exchanges between Job and his friends, Elihu, a much younger man, has been listening (32:11–12). The features of his character are patience, modesty and humility; he does not argue; he does not flatter; he is not partial, but is animated by a spirit of uprightness. He does not set out to prove his own competence, but knows how to identify himself with the poor man who is suffering (33:6–7). What a fine type of the Saviour Who

is to come, the Man amongst men, humbling Himself so
as to be 'among you as one that serveth' (Luke 22:27).

Elihu presents grace, but also truth. He tells Job
straight out what his faults are: believing himself to be
righteous (33:9) and accusing God (33:10–11; 34:5). But
he does not concentrate the patriarch's thoughts upon
himself; he sets before him the LORD.

The younger man stresses the greatness of God
(33:12), Who does not have to account for His actions
(v.13), Who is not unrighteous, but seeks the real good
of His own (vv.14–30).

So Job has to keep silent, to reflect, to stop reasoning
and arguing. Elihu warns him that he is on the wrong
road; the LORD allows discipline so as 'to shew unto
man his uprightness', uprightness in self-judgment,
the only way to blessing and to the knowledge of grace.
But he is aware that it is only God, not man, Who will
make Job yield (32:13).

Elihu again emphasizes the object of this discipline:
to bring the believer to recognise his transgressions,
which have become great, and to turn back from
iniquity (36:8 *et seq*). Two results can be produced:
either to obey and to serve God (v.11) and to find
blessing; or on the other hand not to listen, and to take
the road that leads to misery (v.12).

In concluding his speech, Elihu compares this
discipline to the clouds, to the storm God allows in the
lives of His own: 'With plentiful moisture He loadeth
the thick clouds;...they are turned every way by his
guidance that they may do whatsoever he commandeth
them...whether he causeth it to come as a rod, or for
his land, or in mercy' (37:11–13 JND Trans). Under the
effect of the storm, of discipline, the 'heart trembleth,
and is moved out of his place' (v.1); 'now men see not
the bright light which is in the clouds'. But the purpose
of discipline is blessing: 'the wind passeth and cleanseth

them. Fair weather cometh...' (37:21,22).

The presence of God

Throughout twenty-nine chapters, Job and his friends
have reasoned and argued. Through six chapters, Elihu
has spoken to Job on God's behalf. Four chapters will
suffice for the LORD to bring to perfection the work He
has been pursuing in Job's heart: 'Who teacheth like
him?' (36:22).

Job had said, '...that the Almighty would answer
me!' (31:35). God stoops down. He does not weigh
down His servant with severe reproaches, however
deserved. He takes the place of the pupil: 'I will demand
of thee, and answer thou me' (38:3; 40:2). He will pose a
number of questions to Job, who will be unable to reply
to any of them.

'Where wast thou when I laid the foundations of the
earth?' (38:4). Since the beginning of the interrogation
Job is taken aback. When at last the LORD insists, 'he
that reproveth God, let him answer it' (40:2), Job can
only say, 'Behold, I am vile; what shall I answer thee? I
will lay mine hand upon my mouth. Once I have spoken,
but I will not answer: yea twice, but I will proceed no
further'. It was well to hold his peace, but the LORD
wished to lead His servant further on, right to full
confession and to judgment of himself. So He must
repeat, 'I will demand of thee, and declare thou unto
me!...wilt thou condemn me, that thou mayest be
righteous?'

He has made some of His creatures parade before
him, terminating with leviathan, the crocodile, under
the poetic guise of which we may discern the power of
Satan, the enemy that man is unable to conquer:
'Remember the battle, do no more' (41:8).

Indeed, the LORD intended not only to teach Job to be

silent, but to bring him into contact, into fellowship with Himself. Before the grandeur of the Almighty, he will feel his nothingness and the abyss into which his stubbornness has brought him. What about ourselves, who have received not only the revelation of the Creator, but also that of 'the only begotten Son, who is in the bosom of the Father—he hath declared him'? The better we have learnt to know ourselves, and to turn aside from ourselves, the better we shall know both Himself and His heart (Phil 3:7–10!).

Confession and restoration (Job 42)

Some hundreds of verses tell us how Job had argued, accused God, justified himself. Five verses are enough to recount the confession which is to open for him the way to blessing.

'I know that thou canst do everything, and that no thought can be withholden from thee' (v.2). Confronted with the power of the enemy, Job has to recognise that God's is the only power on which he can depend.

But he must also confess his own ignorance: 'I uttered that I understood not; things too wonderful for me, which I knew not'. He had prided himself on discerning all things, on knowing everything; in the presence of God, he had to declare that he knew nothing. How easily it happens to us that we discourse on matters too wonderful for us, when a little humility would far better become us!

What is Job's conclusion? 'Hear, I beseech thee, and I will speak: I will demand of thee, and declare *thou* unto me!' In silence and in the divine presence, to listen and learn; to allow ourselves to be corrected, instructed, moulded, is not this the portion we often need to seek, apart, alone with Him?

But it is not just a matter of hearing: 'I have heard of

thee by the hearing of the ear: but now mine eye seeth thee': personal and profound experience of the soul, hidden away with his Lord. Vision of young Isaiah in the Temple, which is to set the pattern for his whole life (Isa 6); vision of Paul in the same Temple (rebuilt), when he will hear the voice saying to him, 'Depart, for I will send thee far hence unto the Gentiles' (Acts 22: 17–21).

Job, who had dared to say, 'my heart shall not reproach me so long as I live', declares, 'I abhor myself, and repent in dust and ashes'. He now knows his own heart, but above all he knows God and His grace, 'the end of the Lord, . . . very pitiful and of tender mercy' (Jas 5:11).

The blessing is to be poured out upon the patriarch, finally brought to the point where God wanted him: recognising His greatness and His love: realising his own wretchedness, and abandoning himself to His grace. One thing further had to happen: to forgive his friends. Job prays for them. 'And the LORD turned the captivity of Job, when he had prayed for his friends'. They had driven him to the limit; they had not spoken of God as they ought. They had attributed to God that He had brought a punishment upon their companion. What a lesson to us to be prudent in our judgments! Luke 6:36–37 reminds us of it: 'Be ye therefore merciful, as your Father is merciful . . . judge not, and ye shall not be judged'. The three men must also learn the same lesson as their friend, and be ready to offer a 'burnt offering', so as to be in the good of the same atonement (33:24), which had, in God's eyes, rendered Job 'accepted' (42:8).

The LORD gives Job the double of all he formerly had, except his children. Indeed, if all the former livestock had been lost, the children were not: they, for whom their father had offered the sacrifice, had been taken up into God's presence; they were waiting for the day of that resurrection of which the patriarch had been able to say, 'if after my skin worms destroy this body, yet in my flesh shall I see God; whom I shall see for myself, and mine eyes shall behold and not another' (19:26–27).

2

ELIJAH, JONAH, JOHN MARK

Discipline and restoration to service

The Lord's service exposes us to snares and dangers. The lives of the three men named above provide examples of this. Elijah's ministry was halted by spiritual pride: 'I, even I only, am left'. That of Jonah was shackled by his concern for his personal reputation. John Mark abandoned the work through fear of obstacles and of suffering. But the Father, in His faithfulness, wishes to deliver his servants by discipline from the trap into which they have fallen, and to restore them.

Is is not our part to pray for the Lord's servants, so particularly exposed to Satan's efforts to block their path ('the snare of the devil'—1 Tim 3:7)?

Elijah

The whole ministry of this prophet is marked by the words 'the LORD before whom I stand', repeated more than once in the first part of his career. This communion with God is one of the secrets of his life. —The second is that he was a man of prayer. James 5:17 tells us that 'he prayed earnestly that it might not rain'. Was this not his intrinsic occupation by the brook Cherith? He prays to raise the son of the widow of Zarephath (1 Kings 17:20–21). He publicly calls on the name of the LORD at the altar on Mount Carmel: 'Hear me, O LORD, hear me, that this people may know that thou art the LORD God'. When it is a matter of bringing back the rain, after the people have humbled themselves, 'Elijah went up to the top of Carmel; and he cast himself down upon the earth, and put his face between his knees', seven times over. —The third secret of a service that is blessed: dependence and submission marked his life every time God told him, 'Go' (1 Kings 17:3–8; 18:1; 19:15).

Elijah is an instrument of God's discipline over His people, in order to bring them back to Himself. This discipline is first exercised by years of drought, and then triumphs on Carmel at the confrontation between the prophet of the LORD and the prophets of Baal.

Elijah suffers with God's people. His faith is exercised, first in the solitude of the brook Cherith, then in the simple conditions at Zarephath. At the time of the victory on Carmel, he must stand up alone to the four hundred and fifty prophets of Baal, to the four hundred prophets of the groves, to the king himself and to all his troops. He tells them: 'I, even I only, remain a prophet of the LORD: but Baal's prophets are four hundred and fifty men' (1 Kings 18:22). He was speaking the truth, just as Joshua and Caleb had earlier done, alone confronting the ten spies who disparaged the land, and before all Israel who were weeping.

But what a difference! Those two had been suffering with the people that they had accompanied all across the wilderness. For them this was a school, a time of training, a preparation for the task to which God was calling them; a very different discipline awaited Elijah.

In the prophet's heart a root of bitterness had sprung up: 'I only'. An expression of self-sufficiency, of disappointment with an apparently fruitless ministry, also of pride. What a contrast with the One Who could say, 'I am meek and lowly of heart'. So God's discipline was necessary to lay bare the heart of His servant and to restore him.

The juniper tree (1 Kings 19:1–9)

After the tension of Carmel, Elijah ought to have withdrawn quickly to a quiet place. Fatigue, both physical and spiritual, demanded rest. It is dangerous for a servant of the Lord to have gained a great victory, a fine result to a series of meetings, the approbation of the crowds!...He needs to get into the presence of God, so that the inner man may be totally renewed.

As Elijah has not voluntarily taken this course, he is forced to do so by Jezebel's threats. A long journey of about a hundred and twenty miles, undertaken without prayer, brings him to the south of the country beyond the queen's reach; he flees further still, a day's journey into the wilderness; finally he sits down under a juniper tree and prays for death: 'It is enough; now, O LORD, take away my life; for I am not better than my fathers'. Had he thought that he was? This was the same trap that made Peter stumble: 'Although all shall be offended, yet will not I' (Mark 14:29).

The prophet's career seems to have come to an end. He has given way to discouragement; he now thinks only of death. He lies down and goes to sleep. But God's grace, the Father's discipline, will intervene. At the brook Cherith, the ravens brought bread and meat; in the wilderness an angel was needed to sustain him, and above all to give him his bearings.

The heavenly messenger twice touches him and tells him, 'Arise and eat'; Elijah looks and there, at his head, a cake baked on the coals and a cruse of water. Formerly such a cake had been offered in the Sanctuary, a type of the sufferings of Christ; now, in the wilderness, far from the Temple, far from the altar of sacrifice, it was there to fortify the prophet's soul and to give him the strength to pursue 'the journey that was too great for him'. For forty days and forty nights, in the power of this food, Elijah makes his way to the Mount of God, to the presence of the LORD. The LORD had wished first to strengthen him in the inner man before that memorable encounter when he would be face to face with Himself.

In Job's case it had taken months of wretchedness to lay bare his heart and lead him into the presence of God. For Elijah, it took six weeks. For Jonah, three days and three nights in the depths of the sea. However long it may take, it seems a long time when the soul is not in the enjoyment of communion with his Lord.

Horeb (1 Kings 19:10–18)

In the solitude of the Mount of God, in the same cave perhaps in which Moses took refuge when the LORD passed before him (Exodus 33:23), the divine Word is addressed to the discouraged servant, 'What doest thou here, Elijah?'

The prophet then gives vent to the bitterness of his heart. He accuses the people: 'the children of Israel have forsaken thy covenant, thrown down thine altars, and slain thy prophets with the sword; ... and they seek my life to take it away'. Romans 11:2–4 recalls this incident, as the only fault in a man of God from the Old Testament that is recorded in the New: he makes intercession to God against Israel! What a contrast with Moses who, on the same mount, in circumstances even more grievous, had interceded for the guilty people and would even have wished to offer himself as a ransom for them.

Elijah is not content with accusing others, he also justifies himself; all the spiritual pride of his heart manifests itself: 'I have been very jealous for the LORD God of Hosts...I, even I only, am left'.

The LORD causes all His power in judgment to pass before him: the great and strong wind, the earthquake, the fire,—but the LORD was not in these things. Next comes a still small voice, which Moses had heard in this same place, the voice of grace, unknown to the prophet. The question is repeated: 'What doest thou here?' Elijah begins again, both his accusation and his self-justification. He has not yet understood what God wants to tell him. Discipline has not borne fruit. The LORD's voice must therefore say to him, as once it did to Hagar (Gen 16:9), 'Go, return'.

Return by the way by which thou hast come. Thou hast believed thyself to be the only prophet! I have another prophet in reserve, I have no more *need* of thee; thou art to anoint him, Elisha, son of Shaphat, 'to be prophet in thy room'. —Thou hast believed thyself to be the only one faithful! Well, 'I have left me seven thousand in Israel, all the knees which have not bowed unto Baal'.

What is Elijah's reaction going to be? Is he going to consider himself entirely set aside and, discouraged, go away to spend his days in monotony until his grave is ready for him? No, discipline is going to bear fruit.

Restoration

Without delay, Elijah turns back and finds Elisha. He draws near to him 'and casts his mantle upon him'. Without any jealous thoughts, he lays aside his function as a prophet and transfers it to Elisha. The young man is willing to follow him, but Elijah answers him, 'Go back again', that is to say, I am not asking you to follow me. But Elisha rises up and goes after his master, and will serve him humbly, pouring water on his hands

(2 Kings 3:11). He will be trained by the great prophet of Israel; when God's time is come he will take up again the mantle which, in the time of his youth, had been placed on his shoulders (1 Kings 19:19).

Elijah can again be God's instrument, an instrument full of spiritual energy, to announce to Ahab the judgment that will overtake him on account of the way he has treated Naboth; such a powerful presentation of the Word of the LORD that Ahab humbles himself on account of it and has personal experience of grace (1 Kings 21:27–29). Elijah displays spiritual energy again in the case of Ahaziah the son of Ahab; the prophet is not afraid to denounce his ungodly way, which had led him to call upon Baal-zebub, as if there had not been a God in Israel whose word he could consult.

Finally there was the servant's triumph when, after having retraced all Israel's history from Gilgal to Bethel, from Bethel to Jericho, then beyond Jordan, he did not pass through death but was taken up to Heaven in a whirlwind. Such was God's approbation of the service, the long service, of His prophet.

Jonah

What a strange personality had this man, to whom his own reputation as a prophet was of greater importance than obedience to the call of God (2 Kings 14:25). He backs away from the divine mission, because he fears that it will succeed and that his prophecy of judgment will be overturned! Indeed, if God showed grace to the Ninevites when Jonah had announced the destruction of the City, everyone would be able to say that his prediction was false.

Instead of answering to the call, he flees from the LORD'S presence. He goes down to Joppa, he goes down into a ship, then goes right down into the sides of the ship, where, having lain down, he 'was fast asleep'. What a place for a prophet of the LORD! Discipline will consequently have to be brought into action against him, bringing trouble upon his travelling companions in contrast to the experience of the apostle Paul in Acts 27.

This discipline will take effect in several phases.

First of all the tempest. It has no effect: he is asleep down below.

Then come the questions of the sailors, 'Why hast thou done this?' He had told them that he fled from the presence of the LORD, but he was not much concerned about it, whereas they themselves were exceedingly afraid. The prophet must be brought to confess what he has done: 'For my sake this great tempest is upon you'. Confession is often difficult, but one must not hesitate to make it even before one's brethren when necessary.

Jonah is now in the waves. God's grace makes provision in preparing a great fish for his preservation. For three days and three nights, at the bottom of the sea, from the depths of distress, he is going to cry to the LORD.

Discipline has brought him into the presence of God. Alone in such a situation that he calls it 'the belly of hell', he cries; he cries out of the depth of his distress, he cries from the abyss, from the heart of the seas. In his anguish, when his soul faints within him, he remembers the LORD; his prayer comes in unto Him, into His holy temple. In spite of all, the prophet does not lose his trust in God, and will conclude his supplication with these remarkable words: 'Salvation is of the LORD'.

Will discipline have borne fruit? Alas! Jonah indeed goes to Nineveh; his prophecy touches the consciences of the king and of the people, who repent; the judgment is withheld, God does not make it happen during

Jonah's lifetime. But the prophet finds that very bad, and is irritated by it. He has no understanding of grace, and reproaches God with being merciful and slow to anger.

Then follows the fourth phase of discipline, almost a lesson from infants' school. The LORD prepares a gourd, a castor oil plant, which casts a shadow on the head of our preacher to deliver him from his misery. Jonah marvels at such protection with a naïve joy. Next day the gourd withers; the poor prophet is quite upset by the misfortune of his shrub. The LORD has to say to him, 'Thou hast had pity on the gourd...and should not I spare Nineveh with its hundred and twenty thousand children?'

Jonah is full of solicitude for that which affects him personally, but remains unmoved before the fate of lost souls. In the face of the divine rebuke he is silent. Nevertheless, in His faithfulness, God had prepared everything according to the needs of His servant: the wind, the fish, the gourd, the worm, the east wind. All these had not happened by chance, but were, in God's hand, instruments of His discipline, which the prophet found so difficult to understand and to accept.

The mariners sail away on the calm sea; the Ninevites are delivered from the judgment; but Jonah, annoyed, waits for death. Nevertheless a work must have been done at last in his soul, since, under the action of the Spirit of God, he is not afraid to write his story, and thus to recognise his faults.

John Mark

This young man, too early engaged in service, is stopped by the fear of obstacles and of persecution. What a contrast with the One Who set His face as a flint to go up to Jerusalem, and Who did not shrink from the sufferings He knew He had to meet.

The apostle had said to Timothy, 'Endure hardness' (2 Timothy 2:3); 'endure afflictions' (4:5). There were promises for those who trust in the Lord: Psalm 5:11 tells us, 'Let all those that put their trust in thee rejoice...thou defendest them'. Youthful good intentions are not sufficient reason for engaging in service where perseverance is necessary; love for the Lord is the only motive. Neither the influence of well-intentioned people, nor imitation of other servants, nor a burst of enthusiasm, are enough to make one persevere in this work. It is necessary first to sit down and count the cost before building the tower.

It is good however to pay attention to the encouragements the Lord is able to give, be it directly or through other brethren. Hebrews 10:24 exhorts us to provoke one another to love and good works. In Colossians 4:17 the apostle reminds Archippus to take heed to the ministry which he had received in the Lord, that he fulfil it. In Matthew 21:28 the father tells his son, 'Son, go work today in my vineyard'. In Matthew 20:6 the householder reproaches those who remain in the market place 'all the day idle'.

Young John, surnamed Mark, had nevertheless begun well. In his mother's house (Acts 12:12), under happy influence, he had spent a sheltered youth; in God-fearing surroundings, where prayer was habitual, he had grown up in a good environment. So Barnabas and Saul are able to 'take him with them' when they have accomplished their service at Jerusalem (Acts 12:25). Later he is going to follow them as their 'minister' (Acts 13:5). Accustomed to being waited on (12:13), he learns to serve.

Why, some time later, does he stop and, 'departing from them, return to Jerusalem'? Was it home-sickness for his mother's house, or fear of persecution, or long journeys, or weariness, or difficulties? We are not told precisely, but the Lord had warned His followers, 'No man having put his hand to the plough, and looking back, is fit for the kingdom of God' (Luke 9:62).

So a father's discipline must be brought into action upon John Mark. The Lord wishes him to be set apart for a sufficient time. When Barnabas, in Acts 15:38, wants to take him once more on a journey on which he is to accompany Paul to visit the assemblies, the latter refuses. He discerns that discipline has not yet borne fruit. Barnabas, whose nephew he was, insists and sets out with the young man. This leads to disagreement between the two servants. What results can follow a false beginning! John Mark had yielded thoughtlessly to a passing enthusiasm. The two apostles had perhaps too readily taken the young man as their servant; the consequences now appeared.

Much later, the apostle, a prisoner, will have at his side the same John Mark. He instructs the assemblies to receive him if he visits them (Col 4:10). In Philemon 24, he includes Mark among his fellow-labourers. In 2 Timothy 4:11, he at last declares that he is profitable for the ministry.

What a fine restoration for a man who, instructed and trained by discipline, has been afterwards used by the Holy Spirit, as we understand, to write the Gospel of the perfect Servant.

3

ELI, NAOMI, ABRAHAM

Discipline in the family

Here we see three individuals from former days, each different in character and in family background, and the discipline to which God in His grace subjects them. These far-off happenings are easily transposed into our present-day life; they are quite up-to-date; no great effort is necessary to draw from them some of the lessons God wishes to teach us.

Let us first consider what the Word of God says to us about the *house of the servant of God*. The Bible speaks to us on the one hand about the house of God, and on the other about that of His servant.

As to His house (1 Tim 3:15), God's instructions are clear. It must be marked every day by holiness, spirituality and godliness. God has given its standing in Christ; its practical character depends on the walk of its members. Responsibility here must match privileges, in the joy of a gathering where Jesus is the centre.

The privileges and responsibilities that belong to the house of the servant are also presented in Scripture. In Luke, three passages emphasise it: Martha 'received Jesus into her house' (10:38); to Zacchaeus, quite young in the faith, the Lord says, '*Today* I must abide at *thy* house' (19:5). With the disciples at Emmaus, He allows Himself to be persuaded; 'they constrained him...'. Practical holiness befits the household of the child of God if he realises that the Lord is there. Jacob gives us an example of it (Gen 35:2–3). When God calls on him to go up to Bethel, the question arises: is my household pure to come to the house of God? He says to his family, 'Put away the strange gods that are among you...and change your garments'. Not only Jacob, but his family, had to be ready to answer to God's call and to present themselves before Him.

At the end of his career, Joshua can say, 'As for me and my house, we will serve the LORD'. It is not enough that the father should be faithful; he is called upon to bring his children along with him in the setting of the house of God. —What blessing can result from the faithfulness of a man attached to the Lord: 'The Lord give mercy to the house of Onesiphorus, for he oft refreshed me'.

In 1 Timothy 3:4, the bishop is enjoined to 'rule well in his own house'. No place for worldly vanities, for compromise, for pretentions, for pride. To bring it about, all the grace of God is needed. Applying the exhortation of Revelation 3:20 to the house of God's servant, what encouragement we find to open the door and to allow the Lord to enter, so as to enjoy His precious fellowship in the intimacy of the home.

Eli

Rather an unattractive story and yet so essential at a time when parents no longer dare rebuke nor correct their children!

Eli was much older, it seems, than his sons; this 'age gap' (which can be psychological, not depending on the number of years!) helps to understand certain problems in his family. Moreover, the priest sometimes lacked spiritual perception: he accused Hannah of being drunk when, in her sadness, she sought relief in her prayer of faith (1 Sam 1:13).

His heart was, however, very much attached to the house of the LORD. What a comfort he found in young Samuel, like a grandfather in his godly grandson. Such situations can arise; all the interest, all the joy, are concentrated on the house of God, and one tends to leave the family too often on one side; contact is lost with the children, their interests, their joys, their problems, instead of sharing all these. It is not easy to look after one's family and to concentrate all the time one would wish to the things of God. The Lord alone can be sufficient in this, and can give to His own the necessary balance.

Hophni and Phineas, who did not 'know the LORD', had notwithstanding received the office of priests and served in the house of God. To what end? Essentially for what they could get out of it, as 1 Samuel 2:12–17 demonstrates! The sin of these young men was 'very great' before the LORD, for they despised His offering.

Their misconduct (v.22) caused scandal among the people (v.23). With the years, they had acquired evil ways. But their father seemed unaware of it.

When he learns it (v.22), he says to them gently, 'Why do you do such things? ...Nay, my sons: for it is no good report that I hear'. The father said, 'It is not good'. But the LORD considered their sin to be 'very great'.

Eli, indulgent, tries to intervene by a few words, but he does not apply any correction, any more than he had apparently corrected his sons earlier in life. His example was nevertheless very good. He was a godly man, but lacked firmness; the LORD reproaches him, by the voice of Samuel, with not having 'restrained' his sons when they made themselves vile. No doubt the young men had grown up and had got married (4:19), but the father retained the responsibility, not now to forbid their actions, but at least to restrain them. Solomon, by contrast, gives in his writings many exhortations and reproofs; none-the-less his son Rehoboam did not walk to the glory of God: the king had failed to set a good example.

We truly need God's grace, so that our children may be 'brought up in the nurture and admonition of the Lord' (Eph 6:4). This is quite a programme. To bring up children is not simply to 'let them grow up'. It means sharing with them both the reading of God's Word, with teaching within their capacity, and the gathering around the Lord, at least for the Breaking of Bread; then, when they grow older, for ministry and prayer. It also means associating with them in their various interests, in all the fine experiences that can be enjoyed as a family and which unite parents and children. That is where the parents' example makes itself felt. There is no need for excessive severity: 'Fathers, provoke not your children to anger, lest they be discouraged' (Col 3:21). By being too hard on them one could produce unfavourable reactions, though these might be held in check for a time; and the child's development would be stunted. But this does not imply an easy-going attitude, nor a misplaced indulgence that does not know how to 'restrain'.

Eli's conduct and that of his sons is going to bring about divine discipline. 'There came a man of God unto Eli' (2:27), who spoke to him on behalf of the LORD, stressing among other matters, 'Thou honourest thy sons above me' (v.29). He puts his finger on the fundamental issue: the LORD did not have the first place in this family. Honour and fear were not rendered to Him; the children's satisfaction, their pleasure, came before reverence towards God; their misbehaviour was not restrained. It is easy to neglect the Word in the family, or, on all sorts of pretexts, not to take one's children to the meeting, or even not to go there at all, from time to time. Ought we to be surprised at the results?

Faced with the exhortation of the man of God, Eli says nothing. No repentance; no humiliation. Time passes...the LORD is going to speak once more by means of Samuel, the child brought up in the Temple, whom Eli loves and esteems. The young lad is afraid to pass on the LORD's message to the old priest, but on his insistence he reports the matter to him: 'I will judge his house for ever for the iniquity which he knoweth; because his sons made themselves vile and he restrained them not'. Eli listens and resigns himself: 'It is the LORD, let him do what seemeth him good'. No deeper humiliation is displayed, nor any turning back.

Then the punishment, the disaster, must inexorably take place. Eli's two sons are killed in the battle. When the priest learns that the Ark of God is taken—and not only that his two sons are dead—he falls backward from his seat and breaks his neck. His daughter-in-law, Phineas's wife, gives birth and, in her pains, dies with the words, 'The glory is departed from Israel, because the Ark of God was taken' (4:22).

The old father and his daughter-in-law mark their attachment to the LORD by taking more to heart the capture of the Ark than the death of their son or of their husband; nevertheless the tragedy ends in death, mourning and dishonour.

Elimelech and Naomi (Ruth 1)

A famine arises in the land of Canaan, a trial allowed by the LORD, for a purpose known to Himself. Faith's

attitude would be to search out the reason for this
discipline, to repent, to submit (1 Kings 8:35!). But
Elimelech and his folk do not react like this. They wish
to escape from the trial that God permits, and they run
away to the fields of Moab, beyond the frontiers fixed
by God, initially to 'sojourn' there...very soon they
'dwell' there. The material life of the family is assured,
but everything else is going to be lost. It is as though
they have not merely gone into the world for needed
employment, but they are going to find pleasure in it,
to love it, to settle down in it.

A very up-to-date evolution whereby a change of
atmosphere occurs in many families without their
having to move house. Little by little one conforms to
the world and to the world's things; one finds one's
pleasure in them and...loves them (1 John 2:15).

God's discipline will be exercised first upon
Elimelech, who dies. The widow remains with the two
sons. The young men take Moabite wives who do not
know the LORD. They live there for ten years; they
would have had time to return to Bethlehem. Mahlon
and Chilion die in their turn; 'the woman was left of her
two sons and her husband'. She had apparently been in
agreement at the time with leaving the land and settling
in Moab; then, no doubt, she had not objected to the
marriage of her sons. Should it surprise us that she
must come to the conclusion: 'The Almighty hath dealt
very bitterly with me...the LORD hath testified against
me, and the Almighty hath afflicted me'.

This painful discipline is going to bear fruit. Learning
that the LORD has visited His people to give them
bread, she leaves the place where she was, to return to
the land of Judah. She recognises that she went out
'full'; now the LORD is going to bring her back 'empty'.
But He is going to bring her back. Her heart broken and
humbled, recognising the justice of God's ways without

making excuses, she is going to be a blessing to Ruth, her widowed daughter-in-law, and lead her to come and take shelter under the wings of the God of Israel.

What good relations between mother-in-law and daughter-in-law! Naomi can say, 'Shall I not seek rest for thee, that it may be well with thee?' Ruth will be referred to as, 'thy daugher-in-law which loveth thee' (4:15). Naomi will even find a 'son'; joy will once again fill her heart (4:16).

How shall we set about making our children happy? Not by leading them to 'the land of Moab', but in teaching them to know a Person in Whom is strength: the true Boaz.

Abraham

We do not wish to consider all the patriarch's history, but the fruit produced by God's discipline in his family life.

The call of Abraham was clear: 'Get thee out... from thy kindred, into a land that I will shew thee' (Gen 12:1). But Abraham deviates from the divine instruction: he takes with him his father and his nephew (11:31–32); he goes down to Egypt (12:10); he agrees with his wife to call her 'his sister' (v.13).

The sorrowful consequences of such departures bring upon him divine discipline, but also the precious fruit which that produces.

The father

God's call was not addressed to Terah. No doubt it was hard to leave the old father alone at Ur, but should not faith have been able to count on God to take care of him, as have so many others whom God has called far away into His service since that time? This could have been by means of Nahor his second son. Terah however

accompanies Abraham and his party for the journey to
Canaan; he even appears to take the initiative for it; but
for a reason not given us the troop stops at Haran,
where Terah dies. Only after the father's death 'God
removed Abraham into this land' (Acts 7:3–4).

In this way, a relative can be an obstacle in the path of
faith. A young couple who have set up a home, whilst
retaining respect, esteem and affection for their parents,
especially when these are believers, must accept their
responsibilities and follow the Lord in the path where
faith leads.

Lot

It was no doubt quite natural for Abraham to take his
nephew Lot, the son of his dead brother, with him. But
God's call was not addressed directly to Lot. He followed
on the strength of a faith handed down, under the
influence of the older man.

In going down to Egypt, his uncle does not give him
a salutary example. Indeed, at the time of choice,
resulting from the quarrel between the herdsmen, when
Abraham as the older man allows the younger to make
his choice, Lot lifts up his eyes and sees all the plain of
Jordan 'like the land of Egypt as thou comest unto
Zoar'. Recollections of the Nile country dictate his
choice; he goes away towards this luminous morass
where he will be swallowed up. What an example for
parents who might be tempted to give the taste for
Egypt to their children! These will soon be unable to
recognise the frontiers God has marked out.

What discipline results for Abraham! The sadness of
separation; then his efforts to come to the aid of his
prisoner nephew, with the expense and danger which
are so caused; the anxiety of the patriarch, who
intercedes for Lot when the LORD has decided to
destroy Sodom.

After Lot has lost everything—fortune, home, wife and married children—his daughters deceive him to give birth to the future enemies of Abraham's descendants (Gen 19:37–38).

We may notice what fruit discipline produces for the patriarch, and what sustaining help the LORD gives him. After the separation from Lot, he experiences precious communion with God (13:14); the promises are renewed; at Mamre a third altar is built to the LORD. After delivering Lot from the power of the kings, Abraham benefits from Melchizedek's intervention; the king of righteousness and of peace brings bread and wine, and blesses him on behalf of the Most High God. Thus fortified, the patriarch is able to refuse the insidious invitation of the king of Sodom: 'Give me the persons (the souls) and take the goods to thyself' (14:21). A trap met with by many believers along the way: to set out on a path, in an enterprise, where the children's souls are put in danger, even if the material aspects are secure!

At last, when the LORD is about to destroy Sodom, He appears Himself to Abraham under the oak at Mamre, enables him to enjoy His fellowship, tells him what He is going to do, lends an ear to his intercession and, following this intercession, sends Lot away from the scene of destruction (19:29).

Hagar

From Egypt, Abraham had not only brought back memories, but 'an handmaid, an Egyptian' (16:1), whom he introduces into the intimacy of his family. Here's danger! That there should be in a household some young serving maid who is not a believer is perhaps not ideal, but this does not pose quite the same threat. As against this, to welcome a person or a feature of the world into the circle of intimacy constitutes a permanent danger.

Hagar's presence becomes a cause of tension between mistress and servant, then between husband and wife, not to mention the snare that Sarah's advice has meant to her husband (13:3–6). Later, Hagar having given birth to Ishmael, the boy mocks Isaac (21:9), and introduces a new cause of tension between the parents.

Discipline at last bears fruit: after more than twenty years of communal living, sadly but tactfully, Abraham is obliged to send the slave woman away, to cast her out as it says in Galatians 4:30, so that Isaac may grow up in a peaceful home where faith predominates.

Even the world notices the fruit of this discipline. Abimelech and Phicol his chief captain can say to Abraham, 'God is with thee in all that thou doest' (21:22).

'My Sister'

When God had made Abraham wander far away from his father's house, the patriarch had made an agreement like a 'white lie' with his wife: 'Wherever we get to, say of me that I am your brother'.

This subterfuge had brought about many difficulties during their stay in Egypt (12:14–20). The patriarch, back in Canaan, had been restored to communion with the LORD (13:3–4). But the root of the matter had not been judged: he will again go astray.

In ch 20, Abraham again falls into the same error. This time he at last confesses the deceitful plan that he had agreed with Sarah (20:12–13); he then can pray for Abimelech (v.17) and know full restoration. After so many years, God is able to give him Isaac.

Isaac

Discipline has borne fruit in the life of the patriarch; nevertheless he needs a supreme experience, of which the Word tells us, 'After these things, God did tempt Abraham' (22:1). This was not an experience designed to bring to light some fault and to judge it, but a test suited to make the faith of the man of God shine forth (Jas 2:21). In the tension of these days, Abraham learns to accept all things from God, even Isaac in resurrection (Heb 11:19). He shows the calmness of dignity and faith: 'God will provide himself a lamb for a burnt offering'. This is Jehovah-Jireh. This is the peaceable fruit that the trial has produced, the renewal of the promises, not only to Abraham, but to 'thy seed' (which is Christ: Gal 3:16), in Whom all the nations of the earth are to be blessed, 'because thou hast harkened to my voice'.

4

THE RECHABITES

Personal discipline

The question arises: 'Should we wait "passively" for God's discipline, be it to prevent downfall, or when we have failed?'

The Word shows us in various passages how necessary it is, in dependence upon God's Holy Spirit, to be vigilant and sober, so as to be kept from falling. On the other hand, we are called upon to judge ourselves, recognising and confessing our faults, so as not to be chastened (disciplined) by the Lord, but on the contrary to be led to the joy of forgiveness (Psalm 32).

Discipline, voluntary and preventive (1 Cor 9:24–27; 1 Thess 5:6–8).

For perhaps the tenth time in his epistle, the apostle declares, 'Know ye not...?' This time he is not going to present a doctrine, but rather a practical question: this preventive discipline, so necessary in the race and in Christian warfare. Not legal obedience, but an attitude of heart (Dan 1:8), the result of a work of grace in us which, nevertheless, does not lead us to regard ourselves as superior to others. The secret is to abandon ourselves to grace, so that it may mould us by the action of the Spirit of God, in order to 'mortify the deeds of the body' (Rom 8:13). However, we need to exercise a personal constancy: 'Let us cleanse ourselves from all filthiness of the flesh and spirit' (2 Cor 7:1),—a kind of moral hair-shirt, an effective mortification.

Running and fighting imply a tenacious spiritual energy. In Revelation 2 and 3, in letter upon letter, the Lord repeats, 'He that overcometh...', an individual and personal exhortation, which does not wait for others to have set out on the same path.

Victory in the race or in combat does not come without 'training', in order to obtain a crown (1 Cor 9:25), but also for fear of a fall (v.27).

What does this training amount to? The apostle had personal experience of it: 'I then...', he says. He speaks of keeping his body under, and of bringing it into subjection lest, having preached to others, he himself should be a castaway. This word 'castaway'*, since in this passage it relates to competitive sport, could well be translated 'disqualified'. How could a service for the Lord undertaken in public produce fruit for Him, if we fall badly short of what we preach to others?

Training implies sobriety, that is to say self-control. We see it in 1 Thessalonians 5, where 'those of the day' are seen in contrast with 'those of the night'. In 2 Timothy 4:5, sobriety is necessary to the evangelist. 1 Peter 2:11 enjoins us to abstain from 'fleshly lusts, which war against the soul'. Are not these lusts of the flesh all too often at the root of everything, when a young Christian deliberately turns aside from the Lord's way, invoking as an excuse intellectual doubt, a simple veil for his bad conduct?

Self-control engages the Christian not to yield to all that which surrounds and invites him, or even interests

---

* Greek: dokimos (approved, e.g. 2 Tim 2:15), with prefix 'a': 'adokimos'—disapproved.

him. He is exhorted to keep his 'loins girded' (1 Peter 1:13). The practice of spiritual fasting is called for, particularly in an age when so many things are clamouring for attention. There is no way in which we can hold on to the world's vanities and at the same time to the hand of the Lord.

For love of Him, we should bear His yoke (Matt 11:29). The prophet once pointed out, 'It is good for a man that he bear the yoke in his youth' (Lam 3:27). This yoke of love entails a walk in the same pathway that He walked, following His steps. To set aside ten minutes when we get up for physical exercise, designed to strengthen the body, requires a constant effort. Shall we not each morning employ the same personal discipline, in setting aside enough time to listen to God's Word and to pray to Him? An old booklet had for its title, 'One quarter-hour in ninety-six'—a quarter of an hour to be with the Lord at the beginning of the day. Shall we give Him only one percent of out time? Why not two percent? Shall we spend more time listening to the radio than to His Word? Perhaps that will lead us to give up late nights!

'Forsake not the assembling of yourselves together', says the apostle (Heb 10:25). In this area also we need energy, and a régime that sets apart the necessary time.

The parable speaks to us about 'thorns' (Mark 4:19): cares, riches, lusts, which 'entering in' choke the Word. It is impossible not to have our preoccupations. But we must learn to submit them to the Lord: 'Casting all your care upon him, for he careth for you' (1 Peter 5:7). In an 'affluent society' like that of today, there is a growth of material facilities; we need sobriety to make use of them in accordance with God's mind. He gives us all things richly to enjoy, but to enjoy in the company of the Lord Jesus. As to lusts, let us take care that they do not enter into the soul and do not make war against it.

In so many ways they are fired and fanned by the things we read and hear and see. Many things we cannot help seeing, but we must be vigilant lest they become a part of our inner self.

In Proverbs 24:33–34, we are told, 'Yet a little sleep, a little slumber, a little folding of the hands to sleep: so shall thy poverty come as one that travelleth, and thy want as an armed man'. —What a snare there is in 'a little'—one may have practised sobriety, temperance, but the apostle Peter enjoins us to add to these things patience (2 Pet 1:6), that is to say persevering in sobriety. Not to let ourselves 'just this once' give way to the temptation presented to us. Not to give in 'a little' to the spiritual sleep that lies in wait for us. The enemy would know only too well how to take advantage of it, and so to get a foothold in our life and despoil it.

What consolation we may find in the apostle's affirmation, speaking of the Master's servant, 'Yea, he shall be holden up: for God is able to make him stand' (Rom 14:4).

The Rechabites (Jeremiah 35:1–11; 18–19)

The descendants of Jonadab, the son of Rechab, had received from their father the injunction not to drink wine, not to build houses, not to sow fields, neither to plant vines. Thus they were marked as strangers and pilgrims on the earth. Remember the words of the servant who said: 'Tis the treasure I've found in His love that has made me a pilgrim below'.

Circumstances had become difficult; war had pushed the little tribe into the city of Jerusalem; Jeremiah receives from the LORD the order to invite these men into the temple and to set wine before them. They were to be put to the test. But the Rechabites hold firm. Drinking wine was not bad in itself, but they wanted to obey their father and abstained voluntarily, as he had required them. More than once it is repeated that they 'obeyed' his commandment; the people of Judah, far from following their example, did not 'hearken' to the word of the LORD, and so brought upon themselves the discipline of His chastening (v.17).

It is easy to find the spiritual application of the teaching of Jonadab the son of Rechab. Wine impairs discernment; how many things are inclined to take this spiritual discernment from our minds, if we give way to them. Tents, as distinct from houses, demonstrate that we have not established ourselves in this world, that we do not find our homeland or our satisfaction in it. Not to sow the fields, or to plant vines, means that we do not expect a spiritual harvest from the world, but that we find our joy in the invisible things which are eternal.

The Nazarite of former days (Num 6) abstained from wine and from earthly joys for a set time (Acts 18:18), or for life (Judg 13:5), so as to be set apart for God, entirely for Him. He let his hair grow, renouncing his personal dignity and his reputation,—he refrained from touching any dead person, and kept apart from all corruption. Such a practice was obligatory for no-one, but anybody who, from love of his God, wished to be apart from evil, paid attention to these matters.

Personal discipline when one has failed

1 Corinthians 11:31–32 sets before us a principle of the utmost importance. With regard to the Lord's Supper, we are told, 'Let a man examine himself and so let him eat' (v.28). What does it mean to examine oneself? Just to judge our mistakes? The apostle explains it a little lower down, where he enjoins us to judge ourselves so as not to be judged. Self-judgment implies taking sides with God against ourselves, discerning in the light the deep reasons for our failings. First of all, as we are told

in 1 John 1:9, to confess them, to tell God plainly the wrong we have done, to admit it also to those we have offended. Next, to seek in His presence what were the motives or the underlying reasons for our misdeeds. Thus we shall avoid the discipline the Lord would otherwise have to exercise: 'When we are judged, we are chastened (disciplined) of the Lord, that we should not be condemned with the world'. Much more, we shall be able to say with David, 'Blessed is he whose transgression is forgiven' (Ps 32:1).

Such an exercise will not lead us to a dismal appreciation of matters; on the contrary, it will strengthen in us the feeling of the grace by which we can, in spite of all, draw near for the Lord's supper, to announce His death by which our sins have been blotted out. Let us not say to ourselves, 'This week has not been too bad; I can very well come to the holy table'. Rather let us examine ourselves, judge ourselves, and realise by faith, as if for the first time, that these sins, all too easily present in our ways, have been atoned for at the cross by the Lord Jesus; He has washed us by His precious blood; He is the propitiation for our sins. Then, assured of pardon, and aware of the price He has paid to purge our faults, we come to the table with deep realisation of the immense grace extended to us.

> We know, Lord, Thou hast bought us,
>   And washed us in Thy blood;
> We know Thy grace has brought us
>   As kings and priests to God.
> We know that that blest morning,
>   Long looked for, draweth near
> When we, at Thy returning,
>   In glory shall appear.

Psalm 130:4 tells us, 'There is forgiveness with thee,

that thou mayest be feared'. Awareness of grace does not lead us to recount our faults lightly, but rather to fear to displease the Lord by fresh failure. Proverbs 28:13 teaches, 'Whoso confesseth and *forsaketh* (his sins) shall have mercy'. Does not that call for a serious personal discipline, in the holy desire, by the strength God provides, not to fall back?

PAUL

*Preventive discipline in connection with
the ministry*

Is such discipline really opportune? The numerous
dangers a servant of the Lord is exposed to make us
realise why the Word points out the need for it.

Among these dangers, let us consider that of Romans
12:3: 'To think highly of oneself'! The peril of pride, of
self-satisfaction, which is a pitfall in all public ministry
and at the same time for each individual servant,
whatever his gift of grace or the 'measure' (2 Cor 10:13)
that God has entrusted to him.

In 1 Peter 5:3, the elders are warned not to be 'lords
over God's heritage'; this aspect of lordship might even
weigh upon men's souls, or on other servants (Matt
24:49).

Finally, lassitude is inclined to overcome every one
of the Lord's workers (2 Cor 4). Service becoming
eventually monotonous, above all communion with
God being allowed to lapse, physical or spiritual
weariness, over-taxing the strength which has been
given—all this can lead an otherwise faithful man to
grow weary. Remember that we are servants and not
convicts! In Acts 20:13, Paul desires to go on foot as far
as Assos, leaving his companions to round the
promontory by ship. Did he want to meditate alone
along the road, in precious communion with his Lord?

With regard to these various snares and others like them, the Lord exercises a preventive discipline towards His own; it does not flow from the responsibility of the servant, but from the solicitude of the Master towards those whom He employs in His harvest or in His house.

Paul

Why choose such a servant to illustrate the teaching of the Word on the subject of divine discipline in the course of his ministry? Even the greatest of the apostles had need of it. Let us carefully read again 2 Corinthians 12:5–10, where he himself expresses it.

The essential aim of this discipline was 'lest I should be exalted above measure through the abundance of the revelations'. Throughout his whole career, Paul was the constant, permanent object of this education on the Lord's part, so as to keep his ego in check. The danger was not to have been up to the third heaven, but to 'glory' on account of the revelation received.

Do we not, in our small measure, run a similar risk in respect of the truths brought to light by a ministry that we appreciate, but about which it would be dangerous to 'glory': 'What hast thou that thou didst not receive?' (1 Cor 4:7)?

Three times the apostle beseeches the Lord to take away the thorn that hinders him. But, in the trial, he receives the marvellous answer, 'My grace is sufficient for thee: for my strength is made perfect in weakness'. He can then humbly say, 'I take pleasure in infirmities;... for when I am weak, then am I strong'.

This discipline has assumed two forms: 'A messenger of Satan to buffet him' (2 Cor 12:7), and what he calls 'the sentence of death' (2 Cor 1:9; cf 4:11): opposition from without (persecution), and also from within, in certain assemblies.

The thorn

God had willed to give His servant a thorn in the flesh, and to maintain it despite the apostle's entreaties. The Word has not seen fit to tell us precisely what it consisted of. Several passages mention an infirmity inhibiting his ministry, of which his adversaries took advantage so as to despise him. For example, in 2 Corinthians 10:10 they say, 'His bodily presence is weak, and his speech contemptible'. In Galatians 4:13–14, he wrote, 'my temptation which was in my flesh ye despised not, nor rejected'.

The apostle had learnt to accept such continual suffering from the Lord's hand, aware that He had sent the discipline and was maintaining it. The thorn reminded him that he was only an 'earthen vessel'; if the vessel had wished to play a role, the thorn would soon have put a seal of humiliation on his service.

Let us take care not to despise brothers who have difficulty in expressing themselves, when they truly bring a meaningful message on the Lord's behalf. In Acts 4:13, the apostles were unlearned; their Galilean accent was no recommendation to them at Jerusalem; but the rulers 'took knowledge of them that they had been with Jesus'. Conversely, let us not ourselves be put off by natural difficulties of elocution, or by shyness; but simply, humbly, let us bring what the Lord has given us for the benefit of others.

Persecution (opposition from without)

Writing to the Corinthians, the apostle states that he had in himself 'the sentence of death', so that he should not have confidence in himself, but in God, Who raiseth the dead, and Who was capable of delivering him. He was conscious of 'filling up in his flesh that which was behind of the afflictions of Christ ... for his body's sake, which is the church' (Col 1:24).

In 2 Corinthians 11:23–27, he gives us a summary of these persecutions, endured on so many different occasions, far more numerous than those recounted in the Acts. 'Delivered unto death for Jesus' sake', he could say, 'I take pleasure...in persecutions...for Christ's sake'. Nevertheless he felt them keenly, as witness these lines written to his son Timothy at the evening of his life; 'Thou hast fully known...my persecutions, afflictions...what persecutions I endured' (2 Tim 3:10–11).

The Jews in particular, bitterly hostile to the apostle, made use of persecution to hinder the Lord's work. They had harassed him and his companions by means of it, 'forbidding them to speak to the nations, that they might be saved' (1 Thess 2:15–16). Paul accepted the suffering which resulted from such discipline as coming from the hand of God, sure that the Lord would use it for good: 'The things which happened unto me have fallen out rather unto the furtherance of the gospel' (Phil 1:12). Throughout all these persecutions, all this mortal danger, the life of Jesus was being manifested; a witness was being given to His mighty power. The prophecy of the glorified Nazarene to the one who had so bitterly persecuted the churches ended with these words, 'I will show him how great things he must suffer for my name's sake' (Acts 9:16). The 'earthen vessel' was broken, so that the light within could shine forth.

Exercises and disappointments in the churches (opposition from within)

This opposition from within was much more hurtful to the apostle than all the persecution. Why did he have to endure it, he who was 'called...an apostle of Jesus Christ...ordained a preacher and an apostle...a teacher of the Gentiles in faith and verity' (1 Cor 1:1; 1 Tim 2:7)? And that not only on the part of Judaising teachers, enemies of the truth, but of certain churches and of certain brothers, albeit children of God, having the same faith in our Lord Jesus Christ?

But what would have resulted had Paul been welcomed everywhere? What spiritual danger would he not have run? It was not the Lord's will that it should be so; to maintain His servant in humility, so that he would not be esteemed more highly than his appearance or his reputation deserved, He made him pass through this painful discipline.

His whole heart was committed to the various churches: 'that which cometh upon me daily, the care of all the churches' (2 Cor 11:28). This care even reached out to the churches he had not visited, like Colosse and Laodicea. What profound grief he felt when the Galatians were troubled by emissaries who preached another gospel 'than that which we have preached unto you'. It seemed to him that he 'travailed in birth again for them, until Christ be formed in them' (Gal 4:19). With what sorrow he wrote to them, 'Ye did run well, who did hinder you?' (5:7).

Among the Corinthians, some 'desired an occasion' (2 Cor 11:12) against the apostle. Certain ones found 'his speech contemptible' (10:10). Others had recourse to defamation. Sadly, Paul has to tell them, 'I ought to have been commended of you' (12:11); but such was his affection that he added, 'I will very gladly spend and be spent for you; though the more abundantly I love you, the less I be loved' (12:15).

To the Philippians he speaks of those who 'supposed to add affliction to his bonds' (1:16). But he also knew how to appreciate the encouragements he received from amongst them (1:5,8; 4:1,15–19).

If in our very small measure we have to meet similar

opposition, ought we not to accept the exercise, and seriously consider whether we are really following God's way. If the Lord confirms our conviction, then as earthen vessels we should humbly persevere.

This opposition and scorn which Paul met with in various places had to continue and increase up to the end of his career.

Rejection and loneliness at the end of the race

The apostle when writing to the Colossians (ch 4) already felt this isolation developing. He speaks of certain fellow-servants who were 'of the circumcision', who alone 'had been a comfort to him'. This abandonment was to reach tragic proportions at the end of his life, as described in the second epistle to Timothy.

'All they which are in Asia be turned away from me' (1:15). Amongst them were the Ephesians, known for the highest spiritual level presented in the Epistles.

When Onesiphorus comes to Rome, no-one in the church, so it seems, knew where the apostle was to be found, and could not or did not dare to give directions to the friend who was searching for him. The Ephesian had to multiply his efforts 'very diligently', so as finally to find him and to comfort him on the Lord's behalf.

For the sake of the work, Paul had sent Tychicus to Ephesus. Others had gone away, Crescens to Galatia, Titus to Dalmatia. Demas had forsaken him, having loved this present world. 'Do thy diligence to come before winter', he says to his beloved Timothy. Indeed, 'winter' had already come for the aged apostle in that they were all leaving him.

'At my first answer', he says, 'no man stood with me, but all men forsook me' (4:16). But, for the seventh time in his life, he had the wonderful experience, in a special sense, 'the Lord stood with me and strengthened me...the Lord shall deliver me...and will preserve me unto his heavenly kingdom'.

The fruit of discipline

We shall select six kinds among many others.

1 'We faint not' (2 Cor 4:16). Trained in God's school, renewed every day in his inward man, the apostle was persevering. He remained at the disposal of his Master and of the churches (Phil 1:23–25!), 'faint yet pursuing' (Judges 8:4).

2 The deep conviction of having been given his ministry, 'as we have received mercy' (2 Cor 4:1), upheld him through all difficulties. All service is a grace, and not a hard duty; the discipline through which the apostle had had to pass had made him more deeply convinced of it in his heart.

3 We would at times think after some kinds of service, 'I didn't come through that too badly'. Or we may say with some self-satisfaction, 'The Lord has given us much blessing'!

The apostle himself had had to learn that he was only a worthless vessel: 'We have this treasure in earthen vessels, that the excellency of the power may be of God and not of us' (v.7). Elijah had thought himself better than his fathers, but Paul had realised that he was of no greater value than this earthen vessel destined to be broken.

4 In trial, in persecution, in opposition, he had experienced God's faithfulness, His resources: 'We are troubled on every side, *yet not* distressed; we are perplexed, *but not* in despair; persecuted *but not* forsaken; cast down *but not* destroyed' (vv.8,9). He could also say, 'I am filled with comfort, I am exceeding joyful in all our tribulation' (7:4).

5 All the discipline through which he passed had produced that which in the servant amounts to the

strongest recommendation for it, 'much patience' (6:4).
He had formerly been a great zealot, full of energy in
the defence of God's interests as he imagined them. But
now his unswerving attitude, which commended him
as a servant of God, was this 'much patience... by evil
report and good report... as unknown and yet well
known... as having nothing, and yet possessing all
things' (6:4–10). He could write to the Philippians, 'I
have learnt, in whatsoever state I am, therewith to be
content. I know both how to be abased, and I know
how to abound: everywhere, in all things, I am
instructed...' (4:11–12).

6 At last, as the supreme fruit, the apostle concludes
his epistle by saying, '... though I be nothing' (2 Cor
12:11).

'I am crucified with Christ: nevertheless I live; yet
not I, but Christ liveth in me' (Gal 2:20).

'For me to live is Christ' (Phil 1:21).

'The excellency of the knowledge of Christ Jesus my
Lord, for whom I have suffered the loss of all things'
(Phil 3:8).

Would all this fruit have been produced if Paul had
not endured the hard discipline that had made his
heart bleed, but had thrown him back upon the heart of
God?

Conclusion

What better conclusion to draw from these pages, than that which the Word itself gives us: 'No chastening for the present *seemeth* to be joyous, but grievous: nevertheless afterward it yieldeth the peaceable fruit of righteousness unto them which are *exercised* thereby'.

Job went through it, and at length, but how admirable is his conclusion: 'I have heard of thee by the hearing of the ear, but now mine eye seeth thee' (42:5).

Elijah's spiritual pride, of which he was not aware, has given place, under discipline, to the humility that casts his mantle upon the young man that is to be prophet in his place, although in the order of the three missions God charged him with at Horeb, this was the last to be performed.

John Mark, halted in the work by fear of hardships, becomes, after long discipline, 'profitable...for the ministry'.

The tragedy of Naomi's family results in her returning with Ruth to the land of the God of Israel, and finding the joy of consolation.

Abraham, exercised in his family, in consequence of enduring for a long time the thorns resulting from his aberrations, sees his faith triumph, and the marvellous witness rendered by it to the glory of God.

The Rechabites had listened to their father: they held fast through the long personal discipline in which he had engaged them: God is able to praise them for their faithfulness.

Paul, the great apostle, submissive to the trial by the thorn in the flesh, to persecutions, to opposition from within, displayed great patience and persevered right to the end without giving up, in an increasing communion with his Lord.

Moses had said to the people, at the end of the crossing of the wilderness, 'He has humbled you, He has tested you, He has made you to know His care' ...all that 'to do thee good at thy latter end'.

Is it not true that 'all things work together for *good* to them that love God'?